Lifted Wings

Crystal Dishmon

Presentation by *BookLeaf Publishing*

Web: www.bookleafpub.com

E-mail: info@bookleafpub.com

ISBN: 9789357212724

First edition 2023

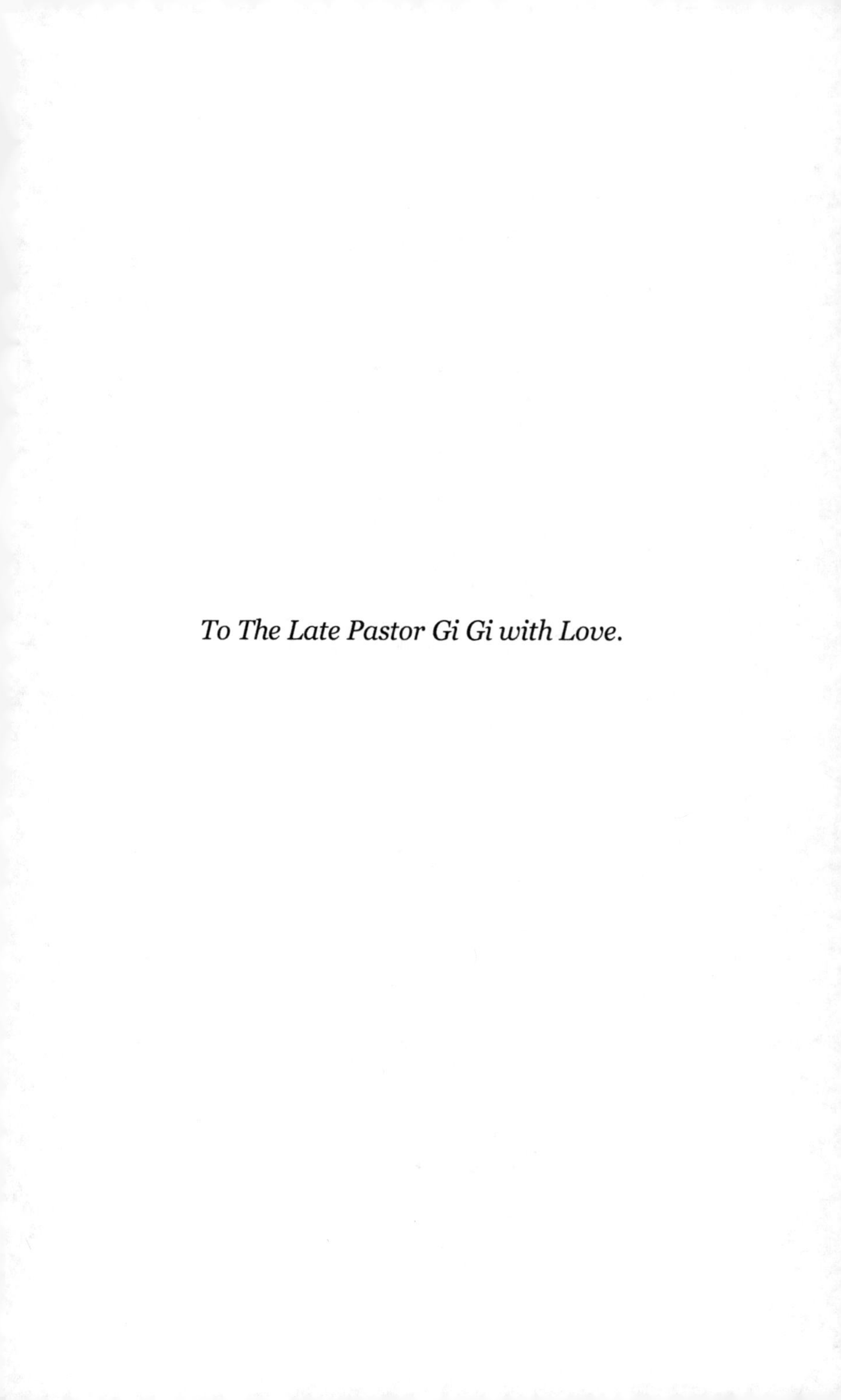

To The Late Pastor Gi Gi with Love.

ACKNOWLEDGEMENT

I want to thank God. I want to thank my wonderful mom, Patricia Dishmon. I want to also thank my family, friends, and all who have supported me throughout my life.

Lifted Wings

The Heavens rejoiced when the Lord said,
Well Done!
The Earth was shattered with heartbreak.
But you said do not cry for you, so we
rejoiced with praise.
You were the chosen vessel that loved us all
so unconditionally.
With our hands raised.
We Thanked God for the angel he created
when he formed you in his own image.
You leave with us your wisdom.
You leave with us your mark.
You leave with us your legacy.
You leave with us your laugh.
You leave with us your smile.
All of which will live in our hearts forever.
The burdens you carried for others.
They have now become your Lifted Wings.
Fly high GiGi, our angel in Heaven.

Black King

I see you Black King with your crown made
of gold.
Symbolic of the land where your ancestors
were born.
The soil of that land runs deep in your soul.
Soul like the blues played down in the deep
south.
Soul like the collard greens, black-eyed
peas, and sweet potatoes cooking on
granny's hot stove.
I see you Black King and you are Royalty.
Royalty like the Queen that gave you life.
You are interconnected with this Queen's
beauty.
While in the womb you were destined to be
great.
So soar on Black King, and know that I see
you.
And although the world turns a blind eye to
your greatness.
Be reassured that you are loved.
And although your crown is cracked, rusted,
and crooked because of what the world has
put you through.
Fix your crown-turn it straight.

Then stand tall, stick your chest out, and
press through.
Cry if you may, because your pain is not
meant to be silenced.
Let your tears flow.
The water from your tears is the libation to
honor your ancestors who cried to be free.
Soar on Black King and know that I see you
with your crown made of gold.

A Heart Created to Love

I have a heart that was created to love.
Like feet were created to walk.
Like hands were created to touch.
My heart was created to love and there is no
need for me to apologize for that.
Therefore, my heart can't stop loving you.
If it does, I may just die a horrible death.
My heart can't help that it's beating so hard-
at a million beats per hour for you.
My heart can't help that it was created to
love you and only you.
Just watch my heart beat for you.
Fall in love with it because it was a heart
created to love you.

Windy My Love (My City)

Your beauty is perfect and a sight worth
seeing.
Our history is so deep, that it cuts real deep.
It's hard to understand why I love you. But
I do.
It's such a tragedy to see how much we have
grown so distant.
I try to get close to you, yet you find more
ways to shatter my heart.
The bloodshed can't be washed away nor
can the tears.
But I will try to move forward.
I will hold on to the Windy, I fell in love
with at 3 years old.
I know she still lives.
Somewhere locked away.
Just waiting to be free again.
Windy my love, you will always be my First
Love.
Windy my love, you will always be (my city).

Treasured Soul

Look into my eyes to search for my soul.
Gaze deep and don't be afraid.
My love will not hurt you.
So search and you shall find.
The treasure key that unlocks the heart to
my soul.
The journey will be rewarding.
I promise, when you find my treasured soul.
You will be so fulfilled, so don't give up the
search.
For my treasured soul.

Pureness

I fell in love with your smile.
I fell in love with your brown eyes.
I fell in love with your beauty inside and out.
I fell in love with your laugh.
I fell in love with your aroma.
I fell in love with the taste of your lips.
I fell in love with the soft tone of your voice.
I fell in love with the pureness of you.
I simply fell in love with you.

Thank you

Thank you for sparking my soul.
The pen to my pad has been unlocked and it
can't be reversed.
Thank you for the voice you helped me to
recreate.
I now use my pen to write down words from
my heart and thoughts from my soul.
I pushed forward, grabbing hold to my
dreams again.
Thank you for the wire you spit through.
It's been my inspiration ever since.

The Black Woman

The Black Woman bears all.
Yet she moves fearlessly.
She is a symbol of courage.
She moves through the world with power
that is so provoking.
She is the rock and the shield.
The Black Woman kneels and prays.
The Black Woman carries the unsolicited
baggage placed on her back by others.
But she still fights through the battles.
The Black Woman is Woman King.

Another Love Language

Shower me with hugs.
Shower me with love.
Shower me with kisses.
Shower me with goodness.
Shower me with roses.
Shower me with time.
Shower me all over.
Shower me forever.
I call this just another Love Language.

Beautiful Affirmations

I'm worth the fight and I'm worth living.
I'm important and especially important to
me.
I have a bright future.
I have so much to offer to this world.
I'm so unique and I'm so creative.
I can push through and I will push through.
I can make it and not give up.
I have a purpose to fulfill.
I'm not going to stop, quit or make excuses.
I see my greatness.
I will let my light shine and not dim it for
anyone.
I desire happiness. I desire peace.
I deserve all of the good things that come
my way.
These are my Beautiful Affirmations.

Ready to Love

I thought I was done with love.
Until I met you.
My feet stalled and my heart was on pause,
because I thought I was done with love.
Then you showed me things I had never
seen when it came to love.
Now I'm convinced that by your presence in
my life, that I'm now ready to love again.

Smile for Me

Your smile is the reason I love you. It's the reason why I care.
Your smile encourages me to never give up and to never fear.
Your smile reminds me to embrace every moment.
Your smile brightens up my day.
So smile for me everyday.

16 Shots

Dead on arrival because of 16 shots.
Just a lost soul wanting to be saved.
Broken and then thrown away.
Left to feel unwanted.
It took 16 shots for his life to matter. Only
his dark soul was left to blame.
For death at his doorstep.
Living in poverty, no one to hold him, and
no hope to hold onto.
16 times his black skin turned into burned
bullet holes.
The city did not own up to their
wrongdoing.
They let his killer walk free.
The people marched in the streets.
Screaming Justice and Peace!
Protesters were silenced by all the bullets
flying everywhere like it was a war zone.
The dreams of the people were overseen by
all the liquor stores on every street corner.
Making dreams easier to bury.
Like the soul lost to 16 shots.

Breathe In Life

Breathe in Life for it's too short to take for
granted.
The seasons come too fast and they don't
last but for a little while.
Take hold of what's yours with no regrets.
Mark the lessons you have learned as
precious time well spent.
Just don't dwell on what could have been.
Life is here for you to experience it.
Breathe it all in, every single bit of it.

Healing Hearts

The hurt feels hard to bear.
You are too hurt to see through all the pain.
Even too hurt to move on, and too hurt to
find a way out.
Depression and sadness may look like they
have won the fight.
But work towards your peace and healing.
The battle you face now will be won one day.
You may never know when.
There is no time stamp on healing.
A Healing Heart just takes time, maybe
more than a lifetime.

Well Wishes

When you left I wished you the best.
I took nothing personal.
You needed to move on, and I needed to
move forward.
There was really no one to blame.
Life granted us the time we had.
Tears were shed.
But I had no other choice but to wish you
well.

Back In Time

I wanna go back in time to when we stayed
at granny's house for the summer.
Pallets of blankets on the floor for sleeping.
All of us cousins were just talking, laughing,
and cracking jokes on each other.
Betting on who will fall asleep first.
So we can get the hot sauce.
When you know you know!
I wanna go back in time to when we played
hide and seek.
Red Light Green Light Stop, jumped double
dutch, and hopscotch.
Those were the times.
When we rode our bikes to the other side of
the neighborhood.
Even though we were only allowed to ride
up the block.
We played in the fire hydrant.
Water blasting so high, all for some cool
summer fun, and when that was done.
We pulled out our super soaker water guns.
Boy those were the days.
I wanna go back in time to when we went to
the park before dark.
We stayed until the street lights came on.

Trips to the candy store were the highlight
of the day.
You get this and I get that! Then we yelled
out no cobbs on my stuff!
I wanna go back in time to when we heard
music blasting from cars rolling down the
block with hydraulics.
We yelled out - That's my car!
I just wanna go back in time to those good
old days.
We had no idea at the time that it would all
fly by so fast.
I just wanna go back in time to those good
old days.

A Prayer Answered

I prayed for you.
Even when I didn't always know what I
wanted.
I still prayed for you.
I only saw you in my dreams.
I imagined you would be like those men I
read about in romance novels.
I wanted you to sweep me off my feet.
So I prayed for you and I prayed for you.
Before I knew it, all my prayers were
answered.
When you showed up in my life just as I
imagined.

Sisterly Bond

What a wonderful bond we have created.
I can call you my best friend through thick
and thin.
You help guide me through this world.
Where would I be without the love you
express to me?
Chances are I would be lost.
You are my hero.
You are the one person I come to for advice.
You are the one person I look to for
motivation.
My sister, my friend, I thank God for you.
I don't ever want this sisterly bond to end.

Shea Butter & Coconut Oil

Love on me like my shea butter does to my
body.
Love me all over just like my coconut oil
glistens all over my melatonin skin.
Smooth like shea butter, is how I want your
love for me to be.
I need a smooth love.
Shine your love on me.
I want it to reflect all over me.
I want you to love me the way I love my shea
butter and coconut oil.

The God of Love

The goodness of my God.
Savior of my life.
The reason why I live.
The reason why no weapon formed against
me propers.
The God I serve is the reason I praise.
The reason why I cry out Hallelujah.
My God is so good to me.
The God of Love is the God I serve
unapologetically.